AMEDEO MODIGLIANI

T&J

Published by TAJ Books International LLP 2012
27 Ferndown Gardens
Cobham
Surrey
KT11 2BH
UK
www.tajbooks.com

All notations of errors or omissions (author inquiries, permissions) concerning the content of this book should be addressed to
info@tajbooks.com.

ISBN 978-1-84406-196-9

Printed in China.
1 2 3 4 5 16 15 14 13 12

AMEDEO MODIGLIANI

T&J

BY SANDRA FORTY

AMEDEO MODIGLIANI

July 12, 1884–January 24, 1920

Amedeo Modigliani was the quintessential suffering artist. He was short—only about 5 foot 5 inches tall—dark and handsome, hugely attractive to women, addicted to drink and drugs, living on almost nothing as he starved and struggled with his art in a Parisian garret. To complete the cliché, he died young, just on the verge of discovery as an artistic genius.

Modigliani's paintings are so linear, spare, and elegant and so very distinctive in style that they cannot ever be mistaken for the work of anyone else. As a consequence, they don't fit into any definable artistic category—his style was his own unique creation. His paintings, which were predominantly portraits and nudes, are instantly identifiable. Interestingly, unlike most of his contempories, Modigliani disliked painting en plein air, much preferring to work inside within the confines of his studio or in a bar or café. In fact, he is only known to have painted three (surviving) landscapes in his life.

After meeting and befriending the Romanian sculptor Constantin Brancusi in Paris, Modigliani took up sculpture for a period. But after 1915, as his strength started to fail, he turned to oil painting. The works he is most famous for—those with his distinctive, elongated, rather flat style—are very similar in approach to his sculptures.

Modigliani's human subjects invariably have almond-shaped eyes with long, slightly twisted noses, small pursed mouths, and elongated necks. The majority of his works are semi-formal portraits that radiate a somewhat sculptural quality, suggesting his early roots as a sculptor. Their faces are expressionless, yet Modigliani infuses them with personality. With his languorous and elongated nudes, he scandalized the polite world. His paintings were considered far too sensual and were viewed as particularly outrageous because they showed body hair, not something that was historically portrayed in fine art.

Modigliani sold few paintings and drawings in his lifetime, more often just giving them away in exchange for a meal or as a token of friendship. After discovering his modernist style, Modigliani destroyed many of his early works, which he viewed as being too academic. Although his work was widely exhibited (especially in France) during his lifetime, he only had one solo exhibition. Upon news of his untimely death, the value of his paintings immediately jumped tenfold.

Amedeo Modigliani was an Italian Sephardic Jew, born in the port town of Livorno on the northwestern coast of Tuscany. The youngest of four children, he lived in a bohemian but literate and philosophical household run by his father Flaminio, a small-time businessman dealing primarily in minerals, and his strong-minded mother, Eugénie Garsin, an avant-garde school administrator and

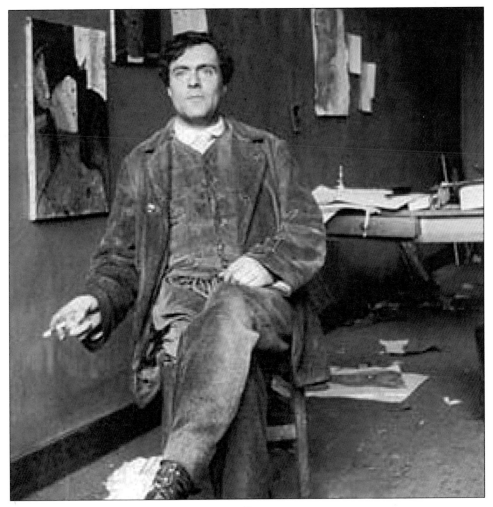

teacher who was a strict but indulgent mother.

The year before Amedeo was born his father was bankrupted following a plummet in the price of metals. The story goes that the bailiffs were about to remove the family's assets, but because an ancient law stated that creditors could not seize the bed of a pregnant woman, the Modiglianis piled as many of their valuables as possible onto Eugénie's bed—she was also said to be in labor at the time.

Modigliani's childhood nickname was Dedo. His mother home-schooled him until the age of 10. In addition, he was well tutored in philosophy and literature by his maternal grandfather, Isaco Garsin, leading to a lifelong interest in radical thinking and idealism. The family home was lively and unconventional, but political views were taken very seriously; in fact, in 1898, Amedeo's eldest brother Emmanuele was imprisoned for six months after being convicted of anarchy.

But Modigliani was never a strong boy. When he was about eleven he had an attack of pleurisy that left him weakened and vulnerable to the typhoid fever he caught a few years later. During that illness he became delirious and raved that he wanted above all else to see the magnificent Renaissance paintings in the Uffizi and Palazzo Pitti in Florence. His worried mother promised faithfully that she would take him there once he was better, and true to her word, she did.

Through his childhood Modigliani drew and painted and showed some talent as an artist. When he turned 14 years old, he was eager to start formal art training under Guglielmo Micheli, the best local painting master and one of the leading lights of the Italian modernist school who had trained under the famous Giovanni Fattori, one of the leaders of the Macchiaioli group of artists. Between 1889 and 1900, Modigliani studied with Micheli and learned the artistic basics with a heavy nineteenth-century classical bent. He studied landscape painting, still life, portraiture, and life studies, at which he predictably—in the light of his later behavior and infatuation with women—excelled. Fattori, the great revered master, would often visit the studio and praise the work of the young Modigliani.

Art lessons stopped when, at the age of 16, Modigliani contracted tuberculosis and was too weak to continue his studies. Instead, in an attempt to rebuild his strength, his mother took him on a lengthy tour around northern Italy, including Capri and Naples, and then on to Rome and the Amalfi coast.

In May 1902, Modigliani left home and moved to Florence where he enrolled at the Scuola Libera di Nudo (Free School of the Nude). He stayed a little under a year before moving to Venice in March of the following year. Again, he enrolled at an arts academy, the Accademia di Belle Arti di Venezia. Venice was a big turning point in Modigliani's life. He began to drink heavily and also to smoke hashish, devoting less time to his studies in favor of experiencing the less reputable aspects of Venetian

Modigliani, Pablo Picasso, and André Salmon, 1916.

life. Among his new companions were Ardengo Soffici and Umberto Boccioni, the leaders of Futurism, a short-lived, intellectual art movement. Together they debated and caroused, and Modigliani increasingly pursued his own philosophy that defiance and disorder were the only way to discover true creativity. These ideas he gathered from his intellectual mentor Nietzsche, whose radical life-affirming philosophies he increasingly supported and tried to follow.

After two years of dissolute living, at age 23 Modigliani announced that he was going to live in Paris, still the center of the artistic world despite the fact that the city was starting to lose its artistic preeminence. He initially rented a tiny studio in Place Jean-Baptiste Clement. Soon he was thrown out because he could not pay the rent. Moving his few possessions—some old clothes, a few books and artist's materials—in a pushcart, he arrived—inevitably accompanied by a woman, Maud Abrantès—in rue Caulaincourt in Montmartre where he moved into an artistic commune called Le Bateau-Lavoir. He maintained the air of a sophisticated but impoverished artist—of an aristocrat fallen on hard times. Modigliani felt it beneath him to do menial tasks to earn money as his other artist friends did, but he made friends easily and his lovers often helped him financially. Pablo Picasso was among his fellow artists in the commune and they became friends—although they did fall out later because of Modigliani's excessive behavior.

During this early time in Paris, Modigliani met and befriended Paul Alexandre, an encourager and supporter of many young artists. Alexandre soon became his patron (much later his memories would be published by his son in *The Unknown Modigliani*). Alexandre immediately recognized Modigliani's brilliance and bought what he could afford from him; sadly, nobody else did.

Around Paris, Modigliani quickly became a notable dandy. An often remarked-upon outfit was a stylish chocolate brown corduroy suit worn over a white unbuttoned shirt with a red bandana at his neck, topped off by a large floppy-brimmed black hat. Picasso is supposed to have said, "There's only one man in Paris who knows how to dress and that is Modigliani."

He wrote home regularly to his mother, and unable to earn anything from his art, he managed to get his mother to agree to give him a modest income, just sufficient to keep him going in Paris. Modigliani was initially thought rather quiet by his fellow artists because he was drinking in moderation and spent much of his time at the Académie Colarossi. There he was quite capable of making up to a hundred drawings a day, but few of these have survived.

By 1906, however, the once-revolutionary Impressionist painters were widely accepted by the art establishment and the avant-garde was looking elsewhere for inspiration. Within a year, Modigliani was drinking heavily—usually absinthe—and smoking large amounts of hashish. His once tidy and classically outfitted studio was a mess. Worse still, he took to destroying his earlier academic paintings explaining that they were "childish baubles, done when I was a dirty bourgeois."

For the first time in his life, Modigliani was introduced to anti-Semitism and, consequently, gravitated toward the Parisian Jewish community for friendship and support. His new friends included the French poet Max Jacob (whose portrait he painted in 1916) and the Cubist sculptor Jacques Lipchitz (who he also painted with his wife in 1916).

In 1914, after years of remission, Modigliani's tuberculosis returned, and his drinking and drug taking escalated. Despite his illness and addictive behavior, Modigliani was an enormous hit with women. He was handsome and louche, conducting numerous affairs, often simultaneously. Many of his lovers were artists' models, such as Lunia Czechowska, but the earliest, most important lover in his life was the 21-year-old Ukrainian poet Anna Akhmatova. They both had a studio in the same building and first met when Anna was on honeymoon. They conducted a year-long affair before she returned to her husband. Modigliani made roughly 20 paintings of her.

Modigliani's reputation for drinking and drug excesses earned him the nickname Modi, which was not just a shortening of his name, but also a pun on the French word *maudit* meaning "cursed." Some of his habits were outrageous; for instance, in social gatherings he was prone to removing all of his clothes when he was drunk. How much of this behavior was genuine and how much of it was an act is unclear, but many observers thought the latter. Certainly Picasso was not impressed. He was famously quoted as remarking, "It's odd, but you never see Modigliani drunk anywhere but at the corners of the Boulevard Montmartre and the Boulevard Raspail."

The most plausible explanation for Modigliani's behavior lies with his tuberculosis. At that time, the disease was a highly infectious killer, spread by coughing and sneezing and thus greatly feared. If people had known of his infection, Modigliani would have been shunned and as a highly sociable man that would have been unbearable. Consequently, his flamboyant use of drink and drugs could explain away his weight loss, erratic behavior, and generally weakened demeanor.

His excesses became too much for his physique, and in 1909 Modigliani returned home to his parents in Livorno to recover and recuperate. But soon back in Paris, Modigliani settled in the Montparnasse area, the new artistic center. At this point in his life he decided to become a sculptor and was particularly inspired by the naïve African and Oceanian works at the Musée de l'Homme and by the elegantly simple work of the sculptor Constantin Brancusi, with whom he became good friends.

Modigliani would wander around the streets of Paris looking for suitable pieces of stone to sculpt—he still had no money so he was forced to steal what materials he could. Luckily, Paris was in the throes of a building boom so there was plenty of stone to be had. His resulting sculptures were of long, minimally elegant, oval heads with straight, narrow noses. Some of these sculptures were exhibited in the Salon d'Automne show in 1912.

His poverty as well as his excessive drinking and drug abuse eroded his health and, once again, in 1912, he became so ill that he had to return to Livorno to recuperate. It was the last time he was to see his old home. But as soon as he was better, he returned to Paris like a moth to the flame. When World War I exploded, the Parisian building boom, which had supplied him with copious amounts of stone, ground to a halt. Thus, finding suitable stone to work became more difficult, even though the

carving and working of the stone had become too demanding for his fragile strength.

Modigliani tried to join the army but was refused on health grounds. So now, instead of sculpting, he turned to portraiture and this earned him a bit of notice. His models were friends and acquaintances and people he saw out and about in Paris. He sold drawings in the bars and cafes in order to get food. In the process, Modigliani made many paintings of contemporary artists living and carousing around Paris including such luminaries as Juan Gris, Picasso, Diego Rivera, and Jean Cocteau.

Around this time he became involved with Emily Alice Haigh, who wrote under the pen name of Beatrice Hastings, a bisexual English poet and critic about five years his senior. They shared an apartment in Montparnasse for two years during which time Modigliani was better fed and cared for, but their tumultuous rows fueled by drug taking and heavy drinking ruined their relationship. One day Modigliani even threw her out of a window, possibly after she tried to castrate him. Their affair was soon over, but she was immortalized in his portraits. Beatrice described him as "a swine and a pearl," remarking that he "never completed anything good under the influence of hashish."

By 1914, Modigliani had established himself enough to have attracted the attention of the ambitious young art dealer Paul Guillaume. The two notably did not get on—even though Modigliani painted his portrait in 1916—so a few years later Modigliani took his paintings to a rival Polish dealer, Léopold Zborowski. The pair became solid friends, and Zborowski allowed Modigliani to use his house as an atelier as well as organized his expositions. Zborowski paid Modigliani a small daily allowance so that he could eat. In total, Modigliani painted three portraits of his friend. Zborowski became a wealthy man through his work with Modigliani and other clients such as Marc Chagall, Maurice Utrillo, and André Derain. Sadly, Zborowski lost all his money in the crash of 1929 and died in poverty in 1932.

One day in July 1917 at the Académie Colarossi where Modigliani liked to draw, he was introduced to Jeanne Hébuterne, the daughter of the noted painter Achille Casimir Hébuterne. She was 19 years old and a beautiful, willowy art student with pale skin, almond-shaped eyes, and long brown hair tied up in braids—an absolute physical ideal for Modigliani. He was 33 years old and reckless. They fell in love and moved together to a shabby apartment on the rue de la Grande Chaumière. Her strict Roman Catholic bourgeois parents were appalled when their beautiful, talented daughter left to live in sin with such a notorious artist. They cut her off as much as her immoral behavior as for the fact that she had fallen for a foreigner and a Jew. Jeanne was noted as being quiet and self-contained most of the time. Modigliani called her his "best beloved," a term he never used for anyone else. He also promised in writing to marry her, although he

never got round to it. They loved each other, but their relationship was tempestuous and often violent, with the pair frequently quarreling in the streets of Paris. They acquired an unenviable reputation for disorderly public behavior. Nevertheless, Modigliani made many soulful and loving portraits of her and she, in turn, loved him unconditionally. Around this time, 1917, Modigliani started painting a series of erotic nudes, pictures that would become some of his best-known works.

The art dealer Zborowski had some success selling Modigliani's work—one nude study went for an astonishing 300 francs—but, on the whole, the paintings were a difficult sell. Modigliani's friend, the writer Francis Carco, bought one of his nudes and hung it in his rooms, and then told the story of how when his cleaner came in to clean the room she was absolutely scandalized by the painting hanging over his bed.

Modigliani's first and only one-man show in Paris opened for a month on December 3, 1917, at the Berthe Weill Gallery. A large nude was placed in the window to advertise the show and it attracted a large, chattering crowd, which was noticed by a policeman from the station across the road. The police chief investigated and was so shocked that he ordered the removal of all the nude paintings. When Berthe Weill demanded to know on what grounds he was acting, he replied, "These nudes . . . they have b-b-body hair!" The exhibition was shut within hours before it had officially opened. Modigliani sold only two drawings.

Due to the ongoing war, life and living in Paris was becoming increasingly difficult, so Zborowski decided to move his business and all his protégés to the comparative safety of the south of France. The idea was that they would sell their work to tourists. Modigliani, despite his increasingly failing health, accordingly moved to Cagnes-sur-mer, near Nice, around the beginning of April 1918. But unlike many of his contemporaries, he found little inspiration or accord in Provence. Perhaps because he came from across the water in Italy, there was nothing exotic or beguiling about the area. Instead of being inspired by the landscape and colors of the Mediterranean, he stubbornly remained indoors, painting portraits of local storekeepers and their children. The south did have some influence on his palette, however, in that his works became somewhat brighter. Most of the paintings he produced were sent to Zborowski in Paris, hoping to sell them, but most of the time he and Jeanne scraped by on little or no money, although he did manage the occasional sale for a few francs a painting. After about July, the couple moved to Nice.

Not long afterward, Amedeo and Jeanne separated for a while, but were together again by the time Jeanne gave birth to their daughter, also called Jeanne, on November 19, 1918. On the way to the Mairie to register the baby, Modigliani got dreadfully drunk and never recorded her as his daughter so baby Jeanne was officially fatherless. Within three

Jeanne Hébuterne

months, Jeanne became pregnant again. On May 31, 1919, at the end of World War I, Modigliani rushed back to Paris, leaving behind his pregnant lover and child.

Throughout the war, Zborowski had been exhibiting Modigliani's paintings, and he was at long last starting to make some progress. Modigliani was getting noticed as a promising artist, and his work was beginning to sell for respectable amounts. A particular success was an exhibition called French Art 1914–1919 held at the Mansard Gallery in Heals department store in the Tottenham Court Road, London, in August 1919. Modigliani showed 59 works, far more than anyone else (including Picasso). For the exhibition's catalog, the novelist and important art critic Arnold Bennett wrote an introduction in which he attacked the insularity of British art and praised the new wave of young French artists, in particular, Modigliani, of whom he said his portraits "have a suspicious resemblance to masterpieces." Bennett was true to his word and paid £60 for the portrait of Modigliani's former lover Lunia Czechowska, likening it to the feelings his heroines were trying to convey. The critics were fulsome. Modigliani was thrilled by the reception his paintings received, but was too ill to journey to London to hear the praise in person.

Meanwhile, that June, now reunited in Paris, Modigliani used the money from the sale of his painting to get his small family an apartment in rue de la Grande Chaumière in a building in which Paul Gauguin had also once lived. Modigliani was collapsing increasingly often due to his alcoholism. He felt that his end was near, nevertheless he continued working—and drinking—until the end. Two weeks into the New Year, Modigliani, weak and emaciated, took to his bed with pain in his kidneys. At some point he caught pneumonia, but Jeanne was so addled with drink and drugs, despite imminently due to give birth, that she didn't call for help. Modgliani is supposed to have whispered to her on his deathbed, "Follow me when I die so that in Paradise you will be there and I will have my favorite model. Together we will share the joys of eternal life."

After a couple of days, a worried friend from the apartment below came to see him and was shocked at his state. Modigliani was clearly delirious and complaining of bad headaches, the apartment was filthy and untidy, littered with empty bottles and covered with opened sardine cans dripping rancid oil. The neighbor immediately sent for a doctor who declared the cause lost, but sent the by-then unconscious Modigliani off to Hôpital de la Charité. He died there two days later on a freezing wet January 24, 1920, without regaining consciousness. He was 35 years old and had died of his old enemy, tubercular meningitis.

News of his passing swept through the art world and hundreds of his fellow artists—including Léger, Derain, Brancusi, and even Picasso with whom he had become estranged—attended his funeral at Père Lachaise cemetery in Montmartre. His tombstone reads, "Struck down by Death at the moment of glory." Modigliani's paintings were suddenly in high demand: it is said that art dealers mingled with the mourners, offering to buy any of the artitst's works that the mourners might be willing sell. Modigliani's old friend, Jacques Lipchitz, cast his death mask, making 12 copies for his friends and family.

All the galleries holding his work at the time of his death raised their asking prices, some as much as tenfold, and the inevitable forgeries appeared as other lesser talents tried to cash in on Modigliani's sudden success. Unfortunately, his family in Livorno had few, if any, of his paintings, and was unable to benefit from his new found triumph. After the funeral, the heavily pregnant Jeanne was taken to her parents' house, but two days later she threw herself out of their fifth-floor window, killing herself and her unborn baby. She was only 22 years old. She was buried at the Cimetière de Bagneux southwest of Paris. Their 14-month-old daughter, Jeanne, received the proceeds of a collection initiated by Modigliani's fellow artists. She was adopted by Modigliani's sister and lived with her in Florence until her death in 1984.

Ten years later Jeanne's family allowed her body to be disinterred and reburied with Modigliani at Père Lachaise. Jeanne, who was a talented and promising artist in her own right—if she had not been overshadowed by Modigliani—would have been much more praised and appreciated today for her own work.

Grave of Amedeo Modigliani and Jeanne Hébuterne in Père Lachaise Cemetery.

13

Plate 1

HEAD OF A WOMAN WITH A HAT

1907 William Young and Company, Boston
35 x 27 cm

THE TUSCAN ROAD

Plate 2

1899 Museo Civico Fattori, Livorno, Italy

36 x 21 cm

Plate 3

BEARDED MAN
1905 Private Collection
42.8 x 26.13 cm

WOMAN'S HEAD WITH BEAUTY SPOT

1906 Private Collection

33 x 24 cm

Plate 4

Plate 5

NUDE WITH HAT
1907 Reuben and Edith Hecht Museum, Israel
80.6 x 50.1 cm

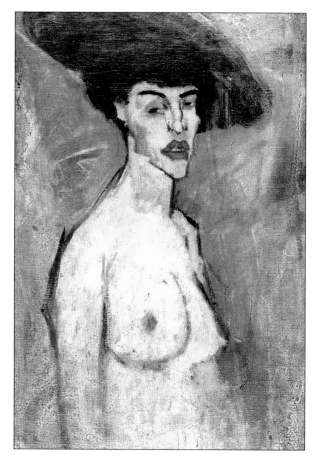

Plate 6

PORTRAIT OF MAUDE ABRANTES

1907 Reuben and Edith Hecht Museum, Israel
Verso of Nude with a Hat

Plate 7

JEAN ALEXANDRE
1909 Private Collection
81 x 60 cm

PORTRAIT OF DR. PAUL ALEXANDRE

Plate 8

1909 Tokyo Fuji Art Museum, Japan
100.5 x 81.5 cm

Plate 9

MAURICE DROUARD
1909 Private Collection
61 x 46 cm

Plate 10

JOSEPH LEVI
1910 Private Collection
53.7 x 48.7 cm

Plate 11

CARYATID
1911 Musée d'Art Moderne de la Ville de Paris, France

STANDING NUDE

Plate 12

1911 Nagoya City Art Museum, Japan
82.8 x 47.9 cm

Plate 13

A RED BUST
1913 Tokyo Fuji Art Museum, Japan
81 x 46 cm

Plate 14

ROSE CARYATID (AUDACE)
1913 The Barnes Foundation, Merion, PA
60 x 45.5 cm

Plate 15

MADAME POMPADOUR

1914 Art Institute of Chicago
60.6 x 49.5 cm

PORTRAIT OF DIEGO RIVERA

1914 Private Collection
100 x 81 cm

Plate 16

Plate 17

PORTRAIT OF FRANK BURTY HAVILAND

1914 Los Angeles County Museum of Art
62.23 x 49.53 cm

Plate 18

ALICE

1915 Statens Museum for Kunst, Copenhagen
78 x 39 cm

Plate 19

ANTONIA
1915 Musée de l'Orangerie, Paris
82 x 46 cm

Plate 20

BEATRICE HASTINGS
1915 Civica Galleria d'Arte Moderna, Milan

Plate 21

MAN'S HEAD (PORTRAIT OF A POET)

1915 Detroit Institute of Arts
46 x 38.1 cm

PORTRAIT OF A MAN WITH HAT (JOSE PACHECO)

Plate 22

1915 Private Collection
65 x 54 cm

Plate 23

PORTRAIT OF CHAIM SOUTINE

1915 Staatsgalerie, Stuttgart, Germany
36 x 27.5 cm

Plate 24

PORTRAIT OF JUAN GRIS
1915 Metropolitan Museum of Art
54.9 x 38.1 cm

Plate 25

ROSA PORPRINA

1915 Civica Galleria d'Arte Moderna, Milan
44 x 27 cm

A WOMAN WITH WHITE COLLAR

Plate 26

1916 Musée de Peinture et de Sculpture, Grenoble, France
92 x 60 cm

Plate 27

FEMALE NUDE

1916 Courtauld Gallery, London
92.4 x 58.9 cm

Plate 28

LOLOTTE (HEAD OF A WOMAN IN A HAT)

1916 Musée National d'Art Moderne, Centre Pompidou, Paris
55 X 35.5 cm

Plate 29

MANUEL HUMBERG ESTEVE

1916 National Gallery of Victoria, Australia
100.2 x 65.5 cm

Plate 30

MAX JACOB
1916 Cincinnati Art Museum
92.7 x 60.3 cm

Plate 31

MONSIER DELEU
1916 National Gallery of Art, Washington DC
146 X 81.1 cm

RECLINING NUDE WITH ARMS FOLDED UNDER HER HEAD

Plate 32

1916 Bührle Collection, Zurich
65.5 x 87 cm

Plate 33

SEATED FEMALE NUDE

1916 Courtauld Institute of Art, London

92 x 60 cm

Plate 34

VICTORIA
1916 Tate Gallery, London
80.6 x 59.7 cm

Plate 35

ADRIENNE (WOMAN WITH BANGS)

1917 National Gallery of Art, Washington DC
55.3 x 38.1 cm

Plate 36

ANNA (HANKA) ZBOROWSKA

1917 Galleria Nazionale d'Arte Moderna, Rome
55 x 33 cm

Plate 37

JACQUES AND BERTHE LIPCHITZ

1917 Art Institute of Chicago

81.3 x 54.3 cm

MADAME GEORGES VAN MUYDEN

Plate 38

1917 Museu de Arte, Sao Paulo, Brazil
92 x 65 cm

PORTRAIT OF ANNA ZBOROWSKA

1917 Museum of Modern Art, New York
130.2 x 81.3 cm

Plate 39

PORTRAIT OF LEOPOLD ZBOROWSKI

Plate 40

1917 Museu de Arte, Sao Paulo, Brazil
107 x 66 cm

Plate 41

WOMAN WITH A BLACK TIE
1917 Musée de l'Orangerie, Paris
65 x 50 cm

MARIE, DAUGHTER OF THE PEOPLE

Plate 42

1918 Kunstmuseum Basel, Switzerland

62 x 50 cm

Plate 43

PORTRAIT OF A YOUNG WOMAN

1918 New Orleans Museum of Art

61 x 45.8 cm

THE ARTIST'S WIFE

1918 Norton Simon Collection, Pasadena, CA
100.3 x 64.5 cm

Plate 44

Plate 45

THE BOY
1918 Indianapolis Museum of Art
92 X 60 cm

WOMAN WITH A GREEN NECKLACE (MADAME MENIER)

Plate 46

1918 Fujikawa Galleries, Japan
99.1 x 59.7 cm

59

Plate 47

YOUNG GIRL SEATED
1918 National Gallery of Art, Washington DC

Plate 48

CYPRESS TREES AND HOUSE
1919 The Barnes Foundation, Merion, PA
60.3 x 45.1 cm

Plate 49

YOUNG WOMAN OF THE PEOPLE
1918 Los Angeles County Museum of Art
89.5 x 64.1 cm

YOUNG WOMAN IN A YELLOW DRESS (MADAME MODOT)

Plate 50

1918 Detroit Institute of Arts
81.5 X 114.5 cm

Plate 51

JEANNE HEBUTERNE IN A YELLOW JUMPER

1919 Ohara Museum of Art, Japan
93 x 54.5 cm

RECLINING NUDE WITH HEAD RESTING ON RIGHT ARM

Plate 52

1919 Galleria Nazionale d'Arte Moderna, Rome
73 x 116 cm

Plate 53

PORTRAIT OF A YOUNG WOMAN

1919 Musée des Beaux-Arts de La Chaux de Fonds, Switzerland
65 x 50 cm

Plate 54

PINK BLOUSE
1919 Musée Angladon, Avignon, France
98 x 63 cm

Plate 55

LUNIA CZECHOWSKA

1919 Museu de Arte Assis Chateaubriand, Brazil
80 x 52 cm

Plate 56

LITTLE SERVING WOMAN

1919 Minneapolis Institute of Arts

92 x 54 cm

Plate 57

GIRL WITH A POLKA-DOT BLOUSE

1919 The Barnes Foundation, Merion, PA

105.2 x 72.7 cm

FLOWER VENDOR

1919 Metropolitan Museum of Art
116.5 x 93.3 cm

Plate 58

Plate 59

GYPSY WOMAN WITH A BABY

1919 National Gallery of Art, Washington DC
115.9 x 73 cm

JEANNE HEBUTERNE
1919 Israel Museum, Israel
54 x 38 cm

Plate 60

Plate 61

LANDSCAPE, SOUTHERN FRANCE

1919 Private Collection

60 x 45 cm

Plate 63

PORTRAIT OF MADAME RACHELE OSTERLIND

1919 Private Collection
46.74 x 33.53 cm

76

Plate 64

ROGER DUTILLEUL

1919 Private Collection
100 x 65 cm

SEATED WOMAN WITH CHILD (MOTHERHOOD)

Plate 65

1919 Musée d'Art Moderne, Lille, France
130 x 81 cm

Plate 66

SELF PORTRAIT
1919 Museu de Arte, Sao Paulo, Brazil
100 x 64.5 cm

Plate 67

THORA KLINCKOWSTROM
1919 Private Collection
99.7 x 64.8 cm

TREE AND HOUSE

1919 Reuben and Edith Hecht Museum, Israel

Plate 68

Plate 69

WOMAN WITH A FAN (LUNIA CZECHOWSKA)

1919 Musée d'Art Moderne de la Ville de Paris, France
100 x 65 cm

Plate 70

YOUNG MAN WITH CAP
1919 Solomon R. Guggenheim Museum, New York
60.9 x 46 cm

Plate 71

A WOMAN WITH VELVET RIBBON

1919 Musée de l'Orangerie, Paris, France
54 x 45.5 cm

BUST OF A YOUNG WOMAN (MADEMOISELLE MARTHE)
Plate 72
c. 1916-1917

Plate 73

BUST OF MANUEL HUMBERT

Plate 74

BUST OF YOUNG GIRL
Musée d'Art Moderne de la Ville de Paris, France
81.5 X 114.5 cm

Plate 75

CHAIM SOUTINE

CONSTANT LEOPOLD

Plate 76

Plate 77

DANCER
Private Collection
55 x 46 cm

Plate 78

SEATED NUDE

Musée des Beaux-Arts, Lyon, France
116 x 73 cm

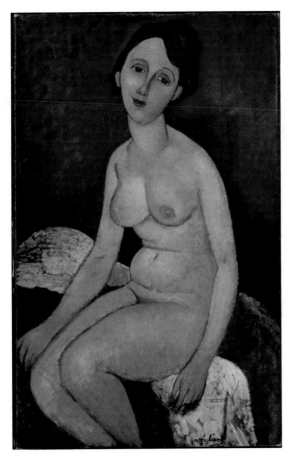

Plate 79

WOMAN WITH EARRINGS

Musée d'Art Moderne de la Ville de Paris, France
65 x 43.5 cm

YOUNG GIRL WITH BLUE EYES

Private Collection

60.9 x 46 cm

Plate 80

Plate 81 YOUNG WOMAN IN A SHIRT (THE LITTLE MILKMAID)
Private Collection
100 x 63 cm

SKETCH OF JEANNE

Plate 82

INDEX